ROLL WITH THE PUNCHES

A True Story of Tragedy and Triumph

To Jada -
You rock! Thanks for having me in your class - I love it! Jess

DEDICATION

I would like to give a shout out to some people who have waited a long time for this book to happen. Get comfy, this might take a while...

First of all, Mom and Dad. You are, and always will be my biggest fans. I would not be half the person I am today without your love and encouragement. You taught me to be strong and confident, to face fear head on, and never let anything stand in my way. Most important, you always lead by example. You support me every step of the way and put up with a ton of my crap and I will never be able to thank you enough.

To Rachel and Jeff. Thank you for always being there for me and for having your needs put aside to accommodate mine so many times. Thank you for always listening and understanding and being my voice of reason.

To Mookie. Thank you for always making me feel beautiful and loved. And for your strength and ongoing support. Thank you for believing in me even when I know you think I'm crazy.

To Lucas and Brayden who will hopefully read this one day. You are my reason for everything always.

To Lindsay for being like my sister, Joan for treating me like a daughter, and to Paul and the rest of my wonderful family. Many thanks to you as well for your understanding and support throughout my journey.

To my best friends, my tribe, the amazing group of women that has weaved their way into my life and never made me feel like I'm different. You listen and laugh and always have my back - Thank you.

And finally, to the many people who have called me an inspiration over the last 24 years. I finally get it.

CHAPTER 1

"Do you smoke?"

Thinking back now, what I was concerned about at that moment seems funny. I was lying on a metal table in the emergency room surrounded by doctors, nurses, my parents, and my boyfriend, who hadn't even taken the time to dress before rushing down. They were all waiting for me to answer the doctor's question: "Do you smoke?"

You would think the answer was obvious, since he was holding a plastic bag with the cigarettes the hospital staff had taken out of my pocket after they cut my clothes off. All I could think about was how mad my father would be if I said yes. How silly it seems now, over twenty years later.

Just an hour before, I was lying in the street pressing my legs with my hands, trying to determine if they were mine or not. I knew they must be, since they were attached to my body, but they were much bigger than mine and I couldn't feel them. I kept asking the woman leaning over me if they were my legs and if they were connected to my body anymore. She was trying to help me calm down and keep still, which would have been a lot easier if she had just answered my question.

I couldn't even begin to comprehend what was happening to me. I was panicked and confused and just wished there was a familiar face to comfort me or anyone who could explain what was happening. The last thing I remembered was a fireman pulling me out of the back seat, and then there I was. I had no idea what transpired from a few minutes earlier when I was smiling in the car with my friends. It almost felt like a bad dream that I would soon wake up from.

But it wasn't. It was just the beginning of a nightmare that fortunately, most people will never experience.

The EMTs put me in an ambulance and whisked me off to the nearest hospital, where they began intense steroid treatment and spinal surgery. I never would have thought on an ordinary day like that one, my entire life would change in the blink of an eye.

I was in a two-door coupe with seven of my friends on our way to our first real girls' night out. We were all young teenagers and really excited to be going out on our own. One of the girls' older sisters agreed to pick us all up and take us to our destination. Being the smallest, I elected to lie across my friends' laps in the back seat.

Right after we picked up the last girl, we were making a left onto a desolate street—that's when I heard the scream. Before I knew what was happening, everything went black. When I came to, I was alone on the floor of the back seat and a fireman was pulling me out of the car, which they had pried open with the Jaws of Life. Later that evening, I learned that my spinal cord had been crushed and I was paralyzed from the waist down.

The whole situation was surreal. This was the kind of thing you would see on an after school special. One minute I was laughing in a car with my friends, and the next, my entire world was turned upside down. In literally the blink of an eye, my entire future was altered.

After an eleven-hour surgery I spent the next nine days in the hospital. On my second day there, one of the surgeons came to speak to me and my parents. While I was being shoved into my cumbersome new back brace, he told me that I would never walk again. I don't remember if it was my mom or dad, but one of them threw him out and I never saw that surgeon again.

I realize now how angry and upset my parents were. They put on a happy face for me, but I could see their tearstains and their puffy red eyes. Obviously my life would never be the same, but neither would theirs. How would they care for me? Would I ever be able to take care of myself? Would I ever fall in love? Get married? Have children? I was their little girl, their first born, their baby. I was suffering, and may very well suffer my whole life, and they knew that there was nothing they could do to help me.

My parents tried so hard to shield me from what was happening. They tried to stay positive and tell me that I would "get better" and together, we would do whatever it took to get me walking again. I honestly never understood how serious my situation was. I thought I was going to be okay. I believed that the nightmare would pass.

I was also completely naïve to the trauma my body had suffered and what it really meant. I don't think I had ever even heard the word "paralyzed" before that day.

A few days later, one of the other surgeons came in to test my nerves and found a reflex in my big toe. He thought this was a great sign and told me I should get to a rehabilitation hospital as soon as possible. The arrangements were made, and for the next four months I would live on the pediatric floor of a rehabilitation hospital in Manhattan, miles away from my home and family and life as I knew it.

I spent the entire first day throwing up. I was so nervous and anxious and wished with all of my being that I could just be home with my family, that I could be in the comfort of my own room and have my mom taking care of me. But I couldn't. My home wasn't my home anymore—at least, for the time being. It was a place that I could no longer physically get into. My room was up two flights of stairs that I could no longer climb. And even if had been able to get to the bathroom, I wouldn't have fit through the door.

I was stuck there, in that cold, strange place. I was a stranger to myself and had no choice but to be alone in a world that was completely unknown.

Living in the rehabilitation center was by far the worst thing I had ever experienced. Don't get me wrong—the physical therapists and doctors were some of the best in their field, but other than that, it was a nightmare. I was away from my family for the first time ever and sharing a room with three other girls who all had their own injuries and problems. One of them was also a paraplegic. She was from Brooklyn and had been at a sweet sixteen party when a fight broke out. Someone pulled a gun intended for their enemy, but the bullet hit her in the back and now we were roommates.

The second girl was also a teenager that had been shot. Her cousin was showing her his gun when it accidentally went off. The bullet went through the front of her neck and came out the back, paralyzing her on one side of her body. She had been there for a while and luckily was almost completely recovered.

The last one of my roommates had a different injury. She was a Hasidic Jewish girl who was also from Brooklyn. She was walking home one evening when a drunk driver crashed into a lamppost on the street next to her. He hit it with such force that it fell over and landed on top of her. She had a long list of injuries, including having her jaw wired shut. The worst of them, which had brought her to the rehab hospital, was having her arm amputated.

Each one of them was a reminder of the instant my life was changed. As different as we were from each other, we now shared this tragic bond. A life-altering event had landed us in that room together. No matter how close we were to others, no one would ever be able to truly understand what it felt like to be "us."

We shared the hospital wing with children of all ages each with their own issues. There were a couple of rooms with "crack babies" and a whole array of children who had been disabled and disfigured. I developed a fondness for a five-year-old boy there and spent much of my free time with him. He was a victim of a drunk driving hit and run. He had lost his ability to walk, talk, and see. He had already been there for several months when I arrived and had gained a lot of his movement back and was learning how to speak again, but he would be there for a long time.

Overall, it was quite the change from my life in the suburbs of Long Island. This was a world unlike any I had ever known, one I wouldn't wish on my worst enemy. The daily struggles and routines we had to endure were nothing I ever want to relive. I spent a lot of time crying. I spent more time wishing I could just leave and go home. I wished to get better, but the more time I spent there, the more apparent it became that that was all it was—wishful thinking.

CHAPTER 2

AT ONE POINT DURING my stay at the rehab hospital, I was sent to a seminar. It was hosted by a group of past patients who had suffered spinal cord injuries and were now living their lives in wheelchairs. They told us how not walking was no big deal and that all of us practicing walking with braces and other assisted devices shouldn't think we were going to put them to any practical use in the future. They are big and cumbersome, and you can't get around nearly as fast.

This was a big setback for me. I was so angry when I left that room. They had taken all of my positive energy and hope and made it seem like something that belonged in a fairy tale. In my mind, it seemed like they thought I was being silly in thinking I was going to be any different than them. They had all been in my shoes, and even if at some point they had hope for a change, it was now gone.

I was devastated. I understand now that they were trying to give us hope for having a brighter future as a wheelchair user, but what a terrible way to get the message across! I left there feeling depressed and defeated, like I had just received awful news and couldn't figure out how to process it. I was in rehab and doing all this work to get better, wasn't I? Why were we trying so hard to learn these things if they were of no use?

This was something I thought about for many years, and it always bothered me. I felt like they had taken away so much of my hope for a recovery or even partial recovery and just wanted me to accept how I was and move on. I didn't want to accept it. I wasn't going to be the average person with a spinal cord injury. I was going to overcome the odds and make miracles happen—I was going to walk again.

One day soon after I was going out to lunch with my mother—we were allowed to leave the hospital for a couple of hours when assisted by a family member. On our way to the restaurant, we passed someone in a wheelchair on a street corner begging for money. It was that day that I said I never wanted anyone to pity me like that. I would never be that person begging for the help of others. Whatever turns my life would take, even if I were confined to a wheelchair forever, I would make the best of it and never expect anyone's pity. I would be someone people respected and never someone that people felt bad for.

I had made my decision—walking or not, I would be a part of society.

CHAPTER 3

EVERY MOMENT I WAS in the rehabilitation center, I counted down the days until I was able to go home again. During my stay, my childhood home was being renovated to accommodate the new me. Before I was actually allowed to leave the hospital, I had to be able to do certain tasks on my own. I had to prove I could get myself in and out of bed, shower alone, cook for myself, and even go food shopping alone. I also had to pass a small obstacle course showing I was able to get up and down a small flight of stairs and different sized curbs on my own. I would have learned to do anything to get out of there, and so I practiced until I was able to accomplish it all. At the end of four long months, I was finally discharged.

When I arrived home after my stay in rehabilitation, it was nothing like the home I had left. I grew up in a split-level house, which would have been completely inaccessible to me had my parents not been able to make several changes. There was now a ramped entrance into the house with an elevator lift to the first floor. There was then a stair lift to go upstairs to the bedrooms. They also had to remodel the bathrooms so I was able to get in and maneuver my way around. Coming back home felt really strange.

It was now my responsibility to start taking care of myself again. I had to get in and out of the shower and the car. I had to get on the toilet and get myself dressed. I was sixteen years old, and on top of all the things I was already concerned about in my life, I also had to deal with this.

As happy as I was to be back home, it was a strange and uncomfortable time. My family treated me just the same except things were just different. It was a physical and emotional adjustment for all of us.

My high school was not ready to take me back yet—they really had no idea how to handle me or my disability. I had to remain home for the rest of the year and be tutored. I wanted my old life back —my friends, my schedule, my old routine. This was definitely one of the most difficult times in my life.

It was at this point I had to make a decision: which road was I going to choose? Should I take the easy way out—stay at home, let my parents take care of me, continue to get tutored, and shun the outside world? Or could I face the world head-on and rise to the challenge? I knew the second choice would be so much harder and scarier, but I also knew if I didn't conquer those fears and make something of myself, I would be miserable. This was the life I was given, and no matter what, I had to live it.

I began learning to do the things I did before, but with my disability. Anything I couldn't find information on, I figured out myself. Living in a time before computers were used and communication was limited to phones and mail, it wasn't such an easy task. I learned how to drive, and of course, how to maneuver my wheelchair in and out of the car. This gave me so much more independence! There were still many places I couldn't figure out how to get into alone, but at least I could get there!

I've had people tell me so many times in my life that if they had been in my situation they would have killed themselves. I know this is a terrible thing to say, but I heard it a lot in the beginning and I still hear it to this day. I always thought it was an awful thing to say, and besides that, saying you would rather be dead than be in my shoes isn't really a compliment, even you're trying to point out how strong I am. The crazy thing is that if I were on the other side, I might have very well said the same thing to someone like me. A year earlier I would have "died" if I had to go to school in an uncool outfit that made me stand out, let alone showing up in a wheelchair!

I think what people don't realize is that we all have an inner strength. Sometimes it just lies dormant until we really need it. I know there was never a time before my accident that I thought I would be able to handle something like this, physically, emotionally, mentally, or in any other capacity. I was self-conscious and always did what I had to do fit in.

I know I was weak. There were many occasions as a child and teen that I can recall where I took the easy way out or played sick or just shied away from things because I was scared. This was different. The decision I made about my new life and my reaction to my new situation would set the tone for my entire future.

CHAPTER 4

I FINISHED MY SOPHOMORE year at home and spent the summer gearing up to go back to school. At that point, pretty much everyone in the school knew who I was and what had happened and that I was coming back. It seemed everyone outside of my circle of friends was curious about me. I knew there would be a lot of attention on me that year, and I tried to prepare myself as best I could. I was so afraid of what people would do and say—I was terrified to return.

Going back for my junior year in high school became one of the hardest steps I had to take since my accident. Being a teenager is stressful enough, and returning to school in a wheelchair took every ounce of courage I had. There were almost fifteen hundred students in my school, and I was the only one in a wheelchair—talk about being a minority!

I wasn't just the only one there in recent memory—I was the only person to attend my school in a wheelchair ever, and the administration really had no idea what to do with me. It was like it was everyone's first day. All I wanted was to blend back in, but I knew there was no way that would happen.

My group of friends and the people I knew well were very supportive. They helped me get around, make it to class, and go out to lunch. I was so thankful for them and everything they did, no matter how small, to make my transition even just a little easier.

There were many students that didn't know me before, but by now, they had heard about me. There were lots of people who tried to be nice and curious kids who just stared at me. Even some of the teachers were clearly uncomfortable, but that was something I was unfortunately getting used to.

There were also some students who liked to make fun of me. Bullying happens everywhere. It is nothing new or uncommon, but no matter what, it's never fun.

I had to have special desks in each classroom. I had to leave classes early because the administration didn't want me in the halls when they were crowded. I had to have a custodian meet me at the elevator—the one they installed for me while I was gone—at certain points throughout the day so I could get to class. I think my favorite was the fire drill routine it took the school months to design. In case of emergency, I was to remain in my class and wait for a custodian or firefighter to come and get me. No student or faculty member was allowed to assist me out of the building.

Each and every day, I was reminded that I was different. As much as I enjoyed my time with my friends in high school, the majority of the time was humiliating and a constant punch in the face. It seemed that the more I tried to fit in, the more I was made to stand out.

I started making plans with my friends again and going out. I tried to put myself out there and realized that my friends and family really didn't care about my disability. No matter how I saw myself, they thought of me as the same person I was before. It took a lot of adjusting and learning for us all to get around and go places, but to my amazement, no one seemed to care. All the people I loved had accepted me for who I was.

As time passed, I continued to grow. I started to feel more sure of myself and was living a "normal" life like anyone else. I had a great time in my college years and enjoyed many experiences that I may not have otherwise had the courage for. I felt I needed to prove to myself and others that I could do anything a "regular" person could do. I just wanted to live life like everyone else.

I joined in a lot of activities at school and started to socialize a lot more. ☐Socializing at that age also involved dating. Dating involved a whole new set of rules and fears that I had not yet faced. I was different than pretty much every girl I knew in a very visible way. There was no getting around it, and I was concerned about how any boy my age was going to want to date me when they could have any other "regular" girl.

I think every teenage girl finds herself at a crossroads at some point when it comes to dating. It is hard for anyone to put themselves out there no matter who they are, but I felt like I had an even bigger challenge. There is so much pressure during that stage of life from peers not only sexually, but in every regard. Even if there was someone interested in me, would they be strong enough to be with me if their friends didn't approve? Teenagers and bullies alike can be relentless, and sometimes it's just easier to forget your own wishes and desires and take the easy way out to please the masses.

Before I met my first boyfriend, there were quite a few awkward scenarios. I never expected everyone to be understanding, but some situations got a little uncomfortable for everyone involved.

One night I was in the back seat of my friend's car going to pick up her boyfriend. When he came outside, he had a friend with him. When they got to the car and opened the door, his friend asked me to move over so he could get in. There was a "hump" in the middle of the backseat and I couldn't really get across without doing some lifting and maneuvering, so I told him I couldn't and asked if he could get in on the other side.

He got annoyed and asked why I was being so difficult (in words that weren't so nice) and asked me again to move over. I told him I really couldn't and when he started to argue with me, his friend quickly explained why I wasn't moving and cleared the air for us both. There was just no easy way out of something like that! He continuously apologized to me throughout the night, which although it wasn't necessary, I understood how he felt. We actually wound up having a great time and becoming good friends.

There was another situation when I was just out of high school that I still recall. There were a group of us that would always hang out together throughout the year. We were all good friends and had a great time together. When school let out, we still remained friends but also had our "summer friends." One of the boys and I were close and spent a lot of time together, even though we were only friends. His summer friends didn't approve; they made fun of him for days. They were teasing him for associating with me and taunting him for thinking I was worth his time. I never knew what was going on until months later when someone else in our group told me. He could have just cut me off, but instead he stood up for me, and more importantly, himself. Things came to a head when he spoke up for himself and got a black eye. I'm not happy it came to that, but I was always grateful.

It didn't take long before I met someone who became my boyfriend and endured all of the awkwardness with me in the dating world. I always needed help going into his house and sometimes had to be carried around. I had to wait while he tried to jam my wheelchair into his sweet little sports car. Even hugging and kissing was different and awkward in the beginning.

I'm glad that I continued to put myself out there. I met so many amazing people, both friends and more than friends. The most important to this day was my husband.

Something that can be very helpful is finding someone in your life that can see in you the things you can't see yourself—a family member, a friend, a mentor, even someone else in your shoes. There will always be times when being positive and enthusiastic can be tough. It happens to everyone, some more often than others. Having a person on your side to give you that little push when you need it can make all the difference. We only have so much strength, and sometimes whatever burdens us can feel like too much to bear. It's nice to have a cheerleader who can bring you up when you feel like you are headed down and can't find your inner strength.

For a very long time, and even now, my parents have been my biggest cheerleaders. They both have two very different ways of dealing with things and with me, but they have molded me into who I am today. My mother was always there for me and always going out of her way to help me. Even when she knew I was physically able to do something but was being stubborn or feeling bad for myself, which happened a lot in the beginning, she would help me. She fought many battles with me and for me, with the schools, the insurance companies, doctors, and I'm sure plenty of people I never knew about. She gave me many pep talks and inspiration and the will to do what so many others said I couldn't. I'm still not sure how, but while she was treating me like her baby and doing everything to make my life easier, she was also helping me build my own inner strength.

My father has always been my silent defender. He has had his own difficulties dealing with my accident and the effect it had on me and our family as a whole. I can't say he was the warmest or most affectionate caregiver, but he has always been just as much of a champion as my mother. He has silently stood by and let me endure the pain I needed to in order to get past my disability. Although we bumped heads many times, he never treated me like I was any different and he never pulled punches. He quietly and resolutely did everything he possibly could to make my life as simple and smooth as it could be while trying to teach me to do the same for myself.

Besides my parents, there have been other who have supported me and assisted me in becoming the person I am today. They have always treated me as an equal. My small group of friends that I have had since childhood that has stood by my side and helped me forget I was any different. There have been many others along the way, but in lieu of sounding like the Academy Awards, I think it's important to acknowledge that there will always be people who believe in you, even when you have trouble believing in yourself.

I would never be where I am today if I didn't adjust to my new self. I was a completely different person on the outside, but on the inside, I was reborn! It was and continues to be a constant battle to face up to my fears. It took a lot of conscious effort on my part to try not to care what people thought of me, or more importantly, only focus on the positive people. I knew my family and friends and even acquaintances with the right outlook would be the best tools I could have on my journey to a better self.

CHAPTER 5

NOT EVERYONE WILL BE as accepting, of course. There have been many times where people, mostly strangers, have made me very aware of my disability. When I was in college, I had a part-time job. Looking for work was always a challenge —not only did I have to be qualified for the position, but I would have to be able to park, get in the building or office, and access the bathroom. Since I was looking for something temporary, I decided to look into retail and filled out applications at a lot of local places.

I went into a large chain drug store very close to my house on the way home one day and decided I should apply there, as well. I asked the girl behind the counter for an application and she asked me, "For what?" I explained I was looking for a part-time job and thought they might be hiring. She said she would give me one but I wouldn't be able to work there because there was nothing I would be "able" to do. I took the application on my way out and the second I reached my car I started crying.

I was so upset by this. No one had ever really told me I couldn't do something before. It wasn't even like this girl had any authority. She was a minimum wage associate who apparently had no common sense or "filter."

When my boyfriend (now husband) came home and saw how upset I was, he told me I should call the corporate office and let them know what had happened—which I proceeded to do. I went through all the channels and got a return call from someone very high up in their corporation. He was extremely apologetic and somewhat embarrassed. He said they had already pulled aside the girl I spoke with and not only reprimanded her, but retaught her their policies on discrimination. He also offered me a job if I still wanted it—I didn't. If she thought that, how many others had thought the same thing? How was it going to be when I started looking for a "real" job? I was completely distraught.

A few days later, I got a call back from somewhere else I had applied to come in for an interview. I was so nervous because that one girl and one statement made me doubt myself and my abilities. Something stupid said by someone who didn't even know me was controlling my whole belief system.

I went for the interview anyway and got the job. It was still just a humdrum part-time position, but I worked extra hard. I wanted to be sure other employees didn't feel I was getting special treatment and knew that I could pull my own weight. Most of the other employees treated me as they did anyone else, but there were some that assumed I got the job out of pity or just ignored me. There were also plenty of customers that wouldn't ask me for help because either they didn't think I could help them or they didn't want to bother with me for whatever reason. I understood not everyone would be comfortable with me. It was something that was just going to be a part of my life.

When I started working at my next job, it was much different. I was hired by a friend of a family member who had just opened a small restaurant. They didn't know me, but of course they knew about my disability before they agreed to hire me. Dealing with the general public was always the same mixed reactions, but whenever there was a rude or ignorant comment, my employers were the first to shut it down or stand up for me. Working for this couple was just as much an experience for me as it was for them.

They gave me a job behind the counter taking orders and ringing people up. They never once treated me any differently than they would have anyone else. They expected me to do my job and treated me with respect. It was actually a little intimidating at first, knowing I wasn't going to be able to get away with anything or give any excuses. After a few weeks there, I was working in all areas of the dining room and doing whatever I could to help out. It was the first time in the work force that I was treated as an equal, and it felt awesome. I have always been so grateful for the opportunity they gave me and the respect they showed me.

For as many people I had on my side, there were still people that tried to stand in my way. There was always someone who didn't think I could do something. I learned that this was going to be a part of my life I would have to learn to deal with. I began to feel like the minute anyone told me I couldn't do something, I had to make a point to do it. I wasn't going to let the word "can't" be a part of my vocabulary. It may not have been the smartest philosophy, but it was how I worked through it.

I never forgot what that girl said to me, even so many years later. It wasn't even what she said, but how she made me feel. How I let the opinion of someone, a total stranger, define me. I almost let her define my reality of who I was and what I could do. It was hard to shake the negative feelings and self-doubt that she left me with, but I did. I learned that I am the only one who can decide what I am and am not capable of.

CHAPTER 6

As I CONTINUED ON with work and school, I also had to find the time to focus on physical therapy. I had never stopped going since my accident and didn't know if I ever would. It too had become a big part of my life and I was still on an ongoing process of trying to find a place that fit my needs and agreed with my beliefs. I wasn't just going in order to stay in shape—I was trying to improve and still hoping to start walking again.

With the support from my family, I set off to looking for a physical therapy office. I didn't want to go to an average place. I wanted something different, something special, someplace that was going to want to help me and give me the attention I was craving.

Finding a place that I wasn't sure even existed was a daunting task. At that time, there still wasn't really an internet to rely on. I had to do a lot of physical searching and trial and error. I traveled around my local area to places I found in the phone book, calling first and setting up appointments.

I was completely bewildered when I showed up to places and couldn't even get in the building!

It took a while for me to realize that physical therapy wasn't necessarily for the handicapped. There were many people who went to therapy for a variety of conditions. It was getting easy to cross different places off my list as I went to scope them out.

At one point, I went to an appointment with a physical therapist I had heard great things about. When I met him he was indeed wonderful, but at my first appointment, the people he had working for him proved otherwise.

I went into a room for my evaluation where two physical therapy assistants met me. They asked me to get up onto the table. On most occasions that wouldn't be a problem, but the table was very high. I explained that I couldn't stand and needed assistance—they gave me a stool. I wasn't sure if they had heard me correctly, so again I told them I couldn't stand up. They said "just use the stool." Apparently I had to spell it out more clearly. I explained that even with the stool, I still couldn't stand. They called in another assistant and we went through the same exact conversation. I decided right then and there I wouldn't be coming back, no matter how good the therapist was.

I eventually found a husband and wife team that were new to the business and quite willing to take me on as a patient, as well as as their newfound research study. She was a physical therapist and he practiced holistic medicine, and together, they were sure they were going to be able to make me walk again—or at least try their hardest.

At the onset of my treatment they began documenting everything I was doing. They had me walking with braces, doing acupuncture, acupressure, weight lifting, balancing—you name it, we did it! I remember one day being in a dark room and having small little incense-like sticks stuck all over my legs and torso doing what was called moxibustion. We were trying everything!

I was feeling very positive! I figured with all of these treatments and experiments, something had to help. Maybe with the combination of all different forms of healing, something would have a conclusive effect, or any effect, for that matter. This was exactly what I had been searching for— people with an open mind who would be willing to try the unknown and hope for the best. I have never been a very black and white kind of person, so venturing into this unfamiliar territory was thrilling for all of us.

I experienced a lot of progress and a lot of success there. I was even able to "walk" with a walker and no braces for very short distances. There were little improvements all around, but nothing phenomenal. My parents continued to support our efforts and even had one of their therapists coming to our house on my days off to work with me.

When it came time for my senior prom, they made sure I was able to at least stand for pictures. I practiced every day standing with the walker and worked until I could stand just holding onto another person. If only for a couple of minutes I would be able to look at a picture of myself standing in a pretty dress next to my boyfriend, then it was worth it. It may seem like such a small thing to most, but for me, it was a huge reward.

I had a lot of confidence and I felt like I could conquer anything, but I still couldn't walk. There were certain things that no matter what I did or how hard I tried, I just couldn't do. I would push myself to the point of tears.

One day while I was at physical therapy, I was working on a particular exercise that I always had trouble with. Both husband and wife were there with me as always, as was the therapist that had been moonlighting at my house on his off days. I started doing a full sit-up, which I was just never able to, most likely because of the lack of stomach muscles. I worked on this exercise every day in therapy and every day in my home for weeks—I just couldn't do it. As they stood around watching, I pushed myself to tears. I pushed and strained and squeezed with every bit of power I had, but I was only able to do a weak crunch—nothing near the sit-up we were all hoping for.

That's when it happened—the husband lost it. He started yelling at me, telling me that I never try hard enough. How would they be able to help me if I wasn't willing to help myself? He was so frustrated—more than I was, at that point. He was so sure that he was going to work a miracle and make me walk again that the only possible reason nothing was working was because of me. Because I wasn't trying hard enough, because I wasn't pushing myself, because I wasn't believing in myself.

At that moment, I was able to see myself through his eyes. I was able to see what the ignorant people who told me "if you worked harder, you would be able to get better" saw. I was looking at myself like a stranger, like someone who just can't comprehend that sometimes it doesn't make a difference how much hope you have or how often you pray. It doesn't matter if you put all the effort you can muster together every minute of every day. There are some things you just can't change.

I have always tried to apply a positive attitude about myself and others, whatever the situation may be. I am a firm believer that positive thoughts and actions bring positive results. Even when you realize that what you are facing is permanent, you have to find a way to live with it. That particular circumstance will not define you, but your reaction to it will. I learned to always try to find the positive in a situation and focus on it, which has helped to create a much better mindset.

CHAPTER 7

I CONTINUED WITH PHYSICAL therapy and graduated high school with my class. I was looking forward to the next step and more independence. After two years, living at home had become much easier and I was happy with the physical progress I had made. But now I was old enough to legally leave my home, and I was determined to conquer that next step.

When I was in college, I was still trying to prove my independence. I wanted to prove to myself, my family, and anyone else who would listen that even though I was thankful for everyone's support, I could still make it on my own. My parents were less than happy about this and fought me with every argument they could rally about me moving out. I'm sure they were just worried about me and how I would deal with the obstacles and emotions I faced each day. I had to go out on my own and see if I could really do it without relying on anyone else. There was no stopping me.

About halfway through my first year, I moved out of my very comfortable home into the dorms at school. I attended college near my hometown, so even though I was leaving, I wasn't going too far. It was a fair compromise.

On one level, it was awesome! I was on my own for the first time ever and had no one to answer to. I had my own room, took care of my own meals, got myself up and ready and off to class every day, and had a busy social life. On the other hand, I had a lot more work to do. I really enjoyed the freedom and all of the choices I had full control of. I also loved the fact that I was really able to manage on my own.

Like any other college student, I also had a lot of anxiety. Since I was living in the dorms and on my own, I thought it would be really cool to join a sorority. It was the time of year for pledging to begin, so I made my rounds to the open houses with my friend and decided which houses I would like to be a part of. This wasn't my hometown and no one really knew "my story," so I didn't know how I would be perceived—especially by an already close-knit group of girls. I was still self-conscious and convinced no one would want me in their group because I would make them look bad. I was very nervous, but I tried to just be myself and hope for the best. My inner voice had me convinced no one would choose me for their sorority.

When the names were picked, I was astonished. I was chosen by three of the sororities. I really couldn't believe it and I have to say it gave me a huge ego boost.

I began the pledging process with my first choice and met an amazing group of girls. A couple of weeks later, though, I decided the sorority life wasn't really for me. I didn't feel it was necessary to go through the measures we were put through in order to belong to a group. As excited as I was and as great as I felt being chosen, I decided to go back off on my own.

As the winter approached, I realized that getting around campus seemed to be my biggest challenge—especially in the snow. The school was spread out, and although it was very pretty, it was not the most accessible place for me to be. Many of the buildings had separate entrances for me to use and some only had one bathroom hidden somewhere that I could get to. Transporting from class to class wasn't very fun, especially when I had to leave the group I was with to enter an alternate way. It wasn't the worst thing in the world, but it was kind of like having all my friends go in the VIP entrance and me having to go through the service door.

When there was snow on the ground, it was an especially difficult task. There were days in the winter I couldn't even get to my classes. That is when I decided that for my lifestyle, living somewhere warm would be very beneficial.

I secretly began looking into other universities in other states. I knew that if my parents gave me such a hard time leaving the house to move twenty minutes away, that moving out of state was going to wreak havoc on my family. I couldn't help it—I had made up my mind. For my own well-being and freedom from the physical barriers I had to deal with on a daily basis where I was, I had to go.

As predicted, I was pretty much the only one who was happy about my decision. My parents were devastated and again tried giving me any reasons they could think of not to go; I didn't have any family there if something happened, the medical care wasn't as good as NY, I couldn't just run home whenever I felt homesick. They also knew by now that if I made up my mind to do something, I was going to do it. I tried to convince them just as I tried to convince myself that I could do it—I could leave my home and family and go off on my own, but I wasn't even sure myself. I just knew I had to try.

I had made the decision to move to Arizona. One of my best friends was going to college there and loving it. I went to visit her for Thanksgiving and decided right then that I had to be there. By the first week of the new year, I had my car packed and was driving across country for the next big move. Again I was terrified, but also very excited. I was hoping for the best, but unsure of how I would handle being so far away from everyone and everything that I knew.

I didn't even realize what a feat this was until now. One of my friends took the ride with me, and together the two of us drove almost three thousand miles—talk about freedom! I may have had a disability, but I was doing so much more than I ever dreamed possible—and more than most able-bodied people would have the courage to do. I truly don't know if this is something I would have done without my disability. I don't think I would have had the courage, or even the desire to leave my comfortable surroundings. I left my support system and every comfort I had for the unknown. It turned out to be one of the best decisions I ever made.

By physically removing myself from everyone and everything that I knew and was content with, I was forced to be my own person. I had no choice but to be independent and handle myself physically and emotionally even on the days I didn't think I could. My family and friends were and continue to be my everything, but taking myself far enough away from them I learned to be my own person and to rely on myself. I know that those close to me were only trying to make my life easier, and they did in so many ways, but I needed this. I needed to know that I could take care of myself.

Being in a warm climate without much rain or any snow really did make a world of difference, as well. The area I was living in was also fairly new, so almost everything was accessible: the parking, the shops, the homes, the bathrooms. It was great! I never got stranded in my house because of weather. I never pulled up somewhere and had to drive away because I couldn't find anywhere to park. I never got somewhere and had to leave because I couldn't get in on my own. I was also able to go visit friends without worrying about being able to get into their homes. It was amazing. I was truly free.

I had so much more confidence in myself than I had before. I was capable, I was happy, I had discovered a whole new way of living. I also ran into my high school sweetheart, who just so happened to live a few miles from where I was. We almost immediately started dating again, and a couple of years later, he asked me to marry him. As much as I missed my family and friends, my life was really in a great place all around, and the next year was amazing.

CHAPTER 8

A LITTLE OVER A year after my move, I was accepted into a research program at The Miami Project to Cure Paralysis where I would be staying for twelve weeks. I was very excited to be a part of what could be very important research. The program was for a "ParaStep" system that used a combination of electrodes and an electronic walker that would allow me to "walk" while by pushing a series of buttons that coordinated with the electrodes. I was going to be walking—this was going to be awesome!

We decided that maybe living near one of the hubs for spinal cord research would be a good thing. I would be able to participate in the program a few days a week and receive physical therapy on the others. My fiancé and I packed up and moved to Miami, hoping for a positive change. I was confident that remaining in a warm climate and in a central area for spinal cord research study would continue to aid in my independence, and I was excited to move again and try someplace new.

About a month after moving, the program began. There was a lot of preliminary testing and training before we actually got started, but I was very happy to be there. I could see and feel the muscles in my legs getting bigger and stronger than they had ever been.

A few weeks into the session, we began walking. It was slow and short at first, only a few feet in several minutes, but as time went on, I was able to walk over a hundred feet in the same amount of time. This was not the normal walking you are used to seeing. It was a very mechanical process. It took a lot of effort and strength, a lot of muscle and sweat, but I didn't care—I felt like Wonder Woman!

I continued to the end of the program, and when the twelve weeks were up, I sadly had to leave the Miami Project. Even more unfortunate was that after leaving the program, there was really no one that was able to help me with the new system. I brought it with me to therapy, I tried doing it at home for a while, but it was just never the same. I was discouraged. I wanted to continue with it, but it just wasn't feasible.

I knew, of course, that I would never be using it as a means to get around, but I loved walking even just for exercise and practice. Trust me, when you are always seeing the world and people around you at waist-level, it's nice to see everything from a different point of view. Yes, I was okay with who I was, but damn, it was nice to be upright again!

Standing and walking through the course of that research was a big eye-opener for me. I realized that this was my life—I was a wheelchair user, I was a paraplegic, but I was still just me. With all the research and medical advances, there was nothing other than a miracle that would make me walk again—at least for now. It was an amazing experience, and it was so good for my heart and soul to be standing and walking for those short periods of time.

But it also brought on the reality I was still having trouble grasping, and I wasn't sure how to process it. In my heart I knew that my situation was permanent, but in my mind I was not willing to accept it and would continue to try and "get better." I believed I would be that miracle, that one in a million person who would beat the odds and defy science. I was scared that once I gave up trying, all hope would be lost.

CHAPTER 9

WHEN I HAD COMPLETED the research program in Miami, I continued physical therapy there and was working in retail. My fiancé had a job, as well, but neither of us really loved living in Florida, so we decided for the time being we would move back home to New York and be with our families while we planned our wedding.

We had our family helping us find a home to rent before we returned. What we discovered was that rentals in an area that was not very transient were somewhat hard to come by, but finding something accessible for me was nearly impossible. Actually, it was impossible. We really had nowhere to go and not many options in our hometown areas, or anywhere close to where we wanted to be.

After much thought and discussion, we made the choice to purchase a home that we could alter and remodel to suit our needs. Apparently, our temporary move was going to become much more permanent.

We drove up the East Coast, headed to our new life back in our old home. I was excited. I had experienced so many new things since I left and we had started a wonderful life for ourselves. I had grown in different ways and discovered many things about myself and my abilities. I knew that if I had to be on my own, I was capable of doing so, but I was content in my relationship and having my man by my side.

We lived with my parents in my very accessible childhood home until we found an affordable one of our own. Once we purchased a home, we had to make several changes to make it usable and comfortable for me, even though it was a ranch house. We had to have a ramp built to get in the side door and both bathrooms modified so I could get in the doors and be able to use the shower and toilet. We also had a deck built in the backyard because even though it wasn't a necessity, I thought it would be nice to be able to go outside and enjoy our own backyard.

After a few months, we were settled into our new home and very comfortable. Buying a house was not exactly what we had intended, but luckily, we were able to afford it and modify it to make it our own. We continued on with our professional lives, working at our respective jobs, and planning our wedding.

Throughout the whole wedding planning process, there was one matter I could not overcome—I wanted to walk down the aisle. I was trying on all these beautiful gowns and veils, and even though I'm sure I'm the only one who noticed or cared, I didn't think anything looked right sitting down. Since I was still going to physical therapy, I expressed my concerns and we decided to practice standing in my leg braces with the walker. If I had a long gown on, no one would be able to see the braces—which was another vain concern of mine—and I would be able to walk, however slowly, down the (hopefully) very short aisle.

I began trying on dresses while wearing the braces, and I felt so much better and so much more confident. I knew it was unnecessary—especially for my soon-to-be husband, who obviously loved me the way I was—but it was how I always pictured myself getting married and I just couldn't see it any other way.

When we were working with the venue for our ceremony, they were very helpful in thinking of constructive ways to make an aisle I wouldn't really have to walk down, but just take a few steps. As beautiful as I felt, I still had on braces and a walker and my walking was very slow. I was also very anxious having to walk in front of all of those people. Until that day, only a handful of my family and friends had seen me upright and walking around, and as much as I wanted to be standing and walking, I was scared to have all of those eyes on me.

It seems ridiculous as I relive the experience in my head: I was too self-conscious to be rolling down the aisle at my wedding, yet I was just as self-conscious to have everyone watch me walk. Honestly, I don't think anyone really cared either way. These were our family and close friends. They were there to share our special day and support our love for each other.

On the actual day of our wedding, we were married on a stage outside. It was beautiful. The venue had set it up so that instead of walking down the aisle and up onto the stage, there was a screened area on stage that looked like part of the scenery. As the guests arrived, no one knew I was sitting behind it, nervous as I could be. When the ceremony started, I mustered every bit of courage I could pull together and with the help of my mom, sister, and best friend, stood up, took a deep breath, and walked out from behind to meet my husband at the altar. No one was expecting it and I think people were either amazed or so happy to see me that way that there wasn't a dry eye in the house. With my bridal gown on and my braces hidden, it was like taking a step back in time. If only for that one day, I could be the woman I had always visualized, it was worth it.

I spent the majority of that day and night on those braces. We shared our ceremony, our first dance, and so many memorable moments that day with me feeling like a true princess. I know many brides say they feel like a princess, but for me, it was just magical. Physically, it probably wasn't the smartest idea; I was used to standing and walking for short periods of time with the braces on, but I didn't care. It took me several days to recover from it, but it was worth every minute.

I guess the point here is that for me, I needed to be standing. I needed to walk down the aisle. I didn't think I looked "right" as a bride sitting down in a wheelchair. I know now that no one else felt that way. No one would have cared how I came down the aisle or danced with my husband. It was me who felt uncomfortable.

It had been ten years already and with all of the courage and strength that had helped me through so many awkward situations, it was like I was wearing a mask. You know the expression "fake it 'til you make it?" That is the best way I can describe how I felt. I would just act like I was okay with myself and my disability until I was cured. Until that day came, I wasn't willing to accept who I was, but I would put on my game face and push myself through each day, no matter what.

CHAPTER 10

FOR A WHILE AFTER we were married, my husband and I continued on with our lives and our jobs. My husband was a chef by trade and I was in business management. We had always talked about opening a restaurant, and when the opportunity arose, we did it. It was not an easy task and took a lot of planning and research, but we plugged along and put in our due diligence to make it happen.

We were able to get a location in our hometown, and together we designed the menu, the wine list, the dining room, and every other detail to make it just how we had always talked about. We had to make some changes due to our actual budget, but it was perfect.

Out of all of the surprises and complications that come with operating any business—especially a restaurant—I was very worried that I had volunteered to manage and run the front of the house. My husband had extensive experience in the kitchen and in restaurants, but me, not so much. I had some business background and I was always a pretty fast learner, but the beginning was like a hurricane. Luckily, I was too busy being caught up in the operations to realize what was going on around me personally.

Since it was our hometown, many of our original customers were people we knew. After a short time as the restaurant received rave reviews and word started to spread, there were people coming from everywhere. I absolutely loved being a hostess—entertaining is my passion. I just never thought about what it was going to be like doing it for strangers who were by no means expecting a girl in a wheelchair to be welcoming and seating them. Although there were many customers who were accommodating and tried not to pay any mind, there were many who weren't.

I'm honestly not sure who felt more awkward —me or them. After so many years I know people are going to stare or look at me different, ask ridiculous questions, or even blurt out odd things, but this was my territory and I wanted to feel comfortable there.

I tried very hard to be nonchalant about everything and just act "normal" when new diners arrived, but it was forced on my part. This was another mask I wore—I was nervous all the time. I was consciously thinking about how I would greet people and carefully planning each move. Even showing them to their table while I carried their menus on my lap was embarrassing for me. We had the dining room set up with enough room that I could get through the spaces and go from table to table, but I still cringed every time I had to do it.

Working the long hours required to operate any business, especially a restaurant, was taking its toll on my body. I didn't complain or make many people aware at the time, but I really had no business working like that for so many hours each day. On top of working, I was still going to physical therapy for treatments two to three times each week. I was overworking myself, but I tried to ignore that so I could maintain everything that I was trying to do. I didn't want to show weakness or have anyone other than me focus on my disability and all of the other ways it made me different.

This went on for years. Even when I was comfortable, it was a vigilant effort. When we were really busy and I had to step in and help out the servers or bartenders, I did my best. There were many occasions where I felt helpless or in the way.

Countless customers commented on how incredible it was that I was putting myself out there like that. It's nice to hear compliments, of course, but it also just pointed out my differences and made me feel that much more uncomfortable. I was always trying to just blend in and do my job, but my differences were continuously being pointed out to me.

I knew that people, for the most part, tried treating me just like anyone else, but my disability was always coming into play. I loved the restaurant business. I loved hosting and serving, but now that I found my career and passion I was very resentful that I had to be different. It was annoying! I had the mental capacity, the desire, and the drive to be good at what I did, but I was always getting held back physically. It was a very frustrating position to be in.

Even with my inner hesitations and struggles, I continued to push on and strive for perfection, because that was still the kind of person I was. I wasn't going to let my inner voice talk me out of something great—I would deal with it.

CHAPTER 11

THE RESTAURANT LIFE TOOK long days and even longer nights. We had an amazing time and my husband and I worked very well together. The restaurant continued to get rave reviews and we were able to keep it going while still enjoying each other and our business. A few years after we initially opened, we started talking about having a family. We both thought we wanted to have children, but I honestly didn't know if it was possible.

My doctors weren't really sure what would happen if I became pregnant, but they did think I would be able to manage, although to what capacity, they were still uncertain. I began to do some research but wasn't really getting anywhere. I searched online and contacted anyone in the spinal cord community I could think of who might be able to help.

With all of those resources, we came upon only one other woman in the northeast with a spinal cord injury who had given birth—twice. I tried to contact her, but was unsuccessful. Our decision to try to conceive was based on this woman we never met or spoke to, who we assumed did fairly well, since she had more than one child. I don't think it was the most educated decision, but it was all we had at that time.

We were lucky and able to become pregnant very quickly. Now that I was actually "with child," I was scared out of my mind. We had no idea what the next nine months (or eighteen years) would have in store for us, and now there was a little baby involved. My gynecologist thought it would be best for us to be with a high-risk practice, so we immediately made an appointment.

The group of doctors there were amazing. Each one was nicer than the next, and all very positive. One of the doctors even said she delivered plenty of babies to paralyzed mothers in her old practice outside of New York and we shouldn't worry. Due to the extensive research we did, I was pretty sure she was making that up, but her enthusiasm was encouraging, none the less. They still didn't know what was going to occur or really what to expect, but they seemed to be looking forward to the challenge. It was going to be another learning experience for us all.

I immediately started to gain weight—partially because I was a lot less active, but mostly because I was eating an enormous amount of food. As my body began to change, I once again had to adjust the way I was getting around, transferring myself, and even driving. I began to fall almost regularly, and unlike before where I was able to lift myself off the ground without much difficulty, I was stuck. I had to call my husband on more than one occasion and say "I've fallen, and I can't get up!" I was still going to physical therapy and trying to keep up with an exercise routine, but every time my body would gain some strength, I would also start to gain more weight and have to start over again.

The doctors were watching me closely, but weren't very concerned about any issues at the time except for my excessive overeating. They had me meet with a nutritionist, who gave me a lecture on proper diet and portions. I had always been a pretty fit and healthy person and was aware of what I was doing wrong—I was just hungry, all the time. She used fake food to give me good examples and had she turned her back, I probably would have eaten those too.

About three months into my pregnancy, I got a call from a friend to watch a documentary that was on one of the science channels about a quadriplegic woman who had her entire pregnancy documented and recorded for our viewing pleasure. Unfortunately for her, about a month into her pregnancy, she began getting dizzy spells. Shortly after, she became unable to sit upright because she would immediately pass out. She spent the remainder of her pregnancy lying in her bed. They showed her right after the baby was born and she was still lying in bed. Fortunately for me, I didn't see this before I decided to get pregnant, because if this was the only reference I had, I would have given it much more thought.

In my fourth and fifth months of pregnancy, things were starting to get much more difficult. I had gone from weighing less than one hundred pounds to about one hundred fifty at that point, and doing anything other than just pushing myself around was becoming a laborious task. Even getting dressed was pretty tough. I had to pull my pants on while sitting down, which I had always done, but I couldn't lift myself that little bit I needed off the chair anymore. Getting myself onto the toilet or into the shower took every ounce of strength I had. I continued to try, and a good portion of the time, I was failing. I was also still working at the restaurant, and that was completely exhausting, even on a good day. To say it was a challenge would be an understatement.

In my last trimester, I was a disaster. Luckily, my health and my baby were right on par, but my body and my physical ability were diminishing. I needed help almost all of the time. I secretly kept hoping the doctors would put me on bedrest so I would have a reason not to move around, but they never did. They told me I was in perfect shape to continue working and going about my daily routines. I felt like my body was under a lot of pressure, and at that point I was carrying around an extra sixty to seventy pounds. I had almost doubled my body weight and I felt like Violet Beauregard from Charlie and the Chocolate Factory, just rolling around like a big, human blueberry.

One Friday afternoon when I was getting ready for work, I noticed a big lump in my bikini area. I knew it was too low to be from the baby, but I also knew it hadn't been there before and I called the doctors' office. They explained that it was probably something pushing on one of my organs and was nothing to worry about. About an hour later, it had doubled in size and I called again. This time I didn't ask questions—I just told them I was coming in. This was a problem, since

Friday night at the restaurant was very busy and I didn't have a replacement. Needless to say, it was a very stressful drive over.

When I arrived at the office and was examined by the doctor, she seemed a little perplexed. The lump had grown even more by then and looked pretty nasty. She thought it was some kind of blood clot and had to slice it open. It was probably one of the grossest medical procedures I had to bear witness to. She made a small incision where the lump was and winced, which is never a good sign from a medical professional. She grabbed some tweezers and one by one pulled out a small cupful of small blood clots that had collected together to form the growing lump. She sewed me back up and sent me back off to work for the night. I was starting to feel like these doctors were giving me way too much credit.

I received a call on Monday informing me that they collectively decided I would have to take blood thinners for the remainder of my pregnancy. They figured my lack of movement and extra body weight might cause another blood clot, which could be a very dangerous situation. I didn't think it was that big of a deal until I learned they were given twice a day by injection. My husband and I went in and learned how to do it and practiced on oranges for a while, but there was no way I was going to be able to stick needles in myself. That was one task I was happy to not have to claim my independence with and gladly let my husband play doctor. Thankfully, he was okay with it and proceeded to give me two shots a day for the next couple of months.

Luckily, that was the worst of it. I trudged along until it was time to give birth. My doctors were hoping I would go into labor and wanted me to try and have a regular vaginal birth, even though they were still unsure if that would be possible. My due date came and went and a week later, I was scheduled for a planned birth.

There were some complications that could happen during childbirth with someone in my condition that could possibly be fatal. The panic I had been holding back finally let loose and as they prepped me for the procedure, I was shaking uncontrollably with fear. Our families must have been pretty scared, as well, because there were more than twenty of them in the waiting room praying and hoping for a success. The doctors induced labor, but my water never broke and after several hours, I wasn't dilating as much as I needed to. They made the decision to perform a cesarean.

Thankfully, everything went just as it should, and a short time later we were introduced to our beautiful baby boy. You could hear the cheering from the waiting room when my husband went out to share the news, and apparently the staff thought we were pretty special too, because they let every one of them in to see us and the baby on our way out of the delivery room.

Just when I thought all the worry and fear I had been carrying around for the last nine months would melt away, a whole new world of uncertainty set in. I had a few days to recover in the hospital and then I would have to figure out how to take care of our child—this little infant that would rely on me for everything. I had no idea what was going to happen or how I would begin to care for him the way he needed to be cared for. As soon as I thought I was past the intimidation of the unknown, I was right back at a new beginning.

I knew I had a lot of support; my husband was amazing and always more than willing to help, and our family lived close by and would be there any time we needed them, but that wasn't good enough. I had to know I could do it on my own. I had to be sure that my son would be able to rely on me from day one and that I would always be able to care for him. I wanted to learn how to accommodate him and suit his needs, and I would figure out a way to adapt to make that happen.

CHAPTER 12

WHEN WE ARRIVED HOME with Lucas, every task relating to baby care was something new we had to learn as parents and I had to change as a disabled mom. I didn't have much experience with babies, either, so there was a lot to get used to. My balance has never been that great, so picking him up was a challenge. Even moving around was difficult—I use my hands to propel myself, as opposed to the average person who walks.

It took a while to master cradling a baby in one arm and pushing with the other—I couldn't just use one hand or I would continue to go in circles. When he grew out of his cradle and moved into the crib, it was impossible for me to reach up and in and get him. I also wasn't able to push myself and the stroller very easily. There were a lot of hurdles to overcome. Fortunately, I love to brainstorm and my husband is very handy.

We started to devise our own devices for making things more accessible. In order to free my hands to hold the baby and move myself around, we designed a carrier I wore on my chest and lap. It allowed me to hold and cradle him, but also kept him safe and secure when I needed to let go and use my hands and arms. My husband disassembled the crib, changed some of the mechanisms, and when he put it back together, it had sliding doors that I could open and reach in at mattress height. We continued to redesign all things baby to make it as simple as possible for me to do what was needed without assistance.

As my baby grew and went in and out of different stages, we too had to grow and adapt. When he started walking and then running, I had a hard time chasing him, especially when he got into places I couldn't go. I always hated those child leashes, but one day when we were playing outside and he stepped down the curb into the street, I knew I would have to get one.

We also designed a foldable handle that was attached to my wheelchair so he could hold on when we were walking or crossing the street— again, I needed my hands to move, so holding his wasn't really an option.

Things constantly changed and progressed, and I continued to adapt and transform to the situations. I can't say it was ever easy, but it was possible. I was a mother now, and I planned on being a good one. I wasn't going to let my differences stand in the way of my care for him or his development. It was a perpetual battle, but it was one I would and still continue to fight. I may not have a choice about my disability but I always have a choice on how it will affect me.

Having a child was a major milestone for me—not just in the way it is for all parents, but it changed something in me. I was a mother now, and I had someone looking up to me as their role model. I knew I would do anything for this child, even if it meant coming out of my comfort zone. It didn't matter how I felt about myself or if I was self-conscious or scared. I would continue to forge ahead so he would always know there was no excuse not to.

CHAPTER 13

BEFORE MY SON REACHED his first birthday, I knew
my time at the restaurant was done. Even if I was
able to put in all the hours and endure the stress,
I didn't want to do it anymore. My husband felt
the same way, and we decided our new family was
more important than our business, so we decided
to sell the restaurant. It was hard to say goodbye,
but we were on a new path.

I got a part-time job and I was still in physical
therapy, but was able to spend a lot of time with
my son. We continued to work and enjoy the
family life for a couple of years before we decided
we would like to have another child.

A short time later, I was pregnant again. This
time around, we were much more confident and
knew what to expect. We decided to try a new
practice that was closer to home. It was still a
high-risk office, but since we didn't think we
were in too much trouble, we didn't see the need
to travel so far for appointments.

Just as the first time, I immediately started to
gain weight. I made it through the first trimester
in good health with a healthy baby. In the
beginning of my fourth month, I started to

experience some bleeding. I went into the office, they ran some tests, and everything was fine. A couple of weeks later, it started happening again. I knew in my heart something was wrong, but again went to the doctor and was told everything was still okay.

A couple of days after, I was bleeding again. I didn't care if I was overreacting; I went back to the doctor. They did some tests and a sonogram, and learned that my baby had no heartbeat.

I was completely devastated. I was at the appointment alone. The doctor sent me home and I just sat in the car in the parking lot and cried for what felt like forever. I called my husband and gave him the news, and of course, he began to cry too.

I eventually calmed down enough to drive, but I was a wreck. I had never felt a pain and sadness so deep. I had never even met this child, but I loved it with all of my heart and soul. I was now over twenty weeks pregnant and carrying my deceased baby.

Because of how far along I was, there wasn't much any doctor could do as far as aborting the child. The only clinic that would perform the procedure turned me away because they were afraid of complications that might arise because of my disability. My only choice was to be put into labor so I could deliver the baby. The horror I felt just thinking about it and visualizing what would occur was inconceivable, not to mention I could not have a natural birth the first time, so I wasn't too hopeful things would go as they planned. One nurse advised me that the only other option would be in an emergency situation. If I experienced bleeding and went to the emergency room, they would have no choice but to do surgery to remove the baby.

I did what I thought was best—I went to the ER and told them I was bleeding. I explained what was going on and they did exactly what the nurse said they would. It may not have been the most honest decision, but it was what I needed to do. I could not fathom watching them pull my unborn, lifeless baby from my womb.

I fell into depression after that. The experience alone was horrific, but since I was already halfway into my pregnancy, I still looked pregnant. I had to endure people continuing to ask me about my pregnancy and when I was due. I then had to deal with the people who already knew I was pregnant, but didn't know what had happened.

For days I had to relive my experience, so I decided I didn't want to leave the house in fear of having to tell the story yet again. It was a very dark time for me and it was probably the first time I wasn't sure where how to pull myself together.

It took a couple of weeks, but I did. I did it for me and I did it for my son, who did not deserve to deal with me in that state. I dealt with it and I mourned and then I picked my head up and faced the world again. That's what life was all about, wasn't it? I hadn't let anything hold me back before, and I wasn't about to start now.

CHAPTER 14

I'M NOT REALLY SURE when or how the decision was made, but it was. A couple of years later, my husband and I decided to go back into business again. We didn't want the long, grueling hours of a restaurant and decided a deli and catering business might be a better way to go. We researched some areas and different places for sale and found an affordable little spot a few miles from our home.

We began the whole process again—designing menus and logos, arranging equipment, and doing whatever else we could to make the tiny place work. Shortly before we opened, we learned I was pregnant again. It took me a long time to overcome the last pregnancy, and even though I knew there was no apparent reason for it, I was scared this time.

We went back to our original practice, and this time it was a smoother process. They had a better idea of what to expect, and since I had a C-section with my firstborn, I would be having one scheduled again this time. They also had me immediately start blood thinner injections to avoid any complications with clotting.

Although I started to gain a lot of weight again, my first trimester was pretty uneventful. As I started to get bigger, it also started to become harder to get around again—especially with another child to take care of. I think it is pretty difficult for any woman to juggle being pregnant with a job and a child, and I will admit, it was becoming more of a challenge each day.

My physical space at work was limited to begin with, and moving around was tough, even more so as I grew. My job was somewhat physical, and bending down and picking things up was almost impossible, but I had to do everything I could to keep up. I didn't want to be different or be treated that way by anyone. I was lucky that my four-year-old was pretty independent and loved to help me out when he could. I wasn't able to pick him up anymore, but he was able to climb onto the small piece of lap I had left that wasn't covered by my giant belly!

During my fifth and sixth months, I started falling again. I didn't have the strength I needed to lift myself from one place to another and just had to concede and fall to the floor. I had learned to fall as slowly and gracefully as one can, but I would wind up on the floor regardless. It resulted in me having to call my husband or mom, or anyone who would be able to assist me back up.

One night when I was almost seven months pregnant, I was taking a shower. I use a plastic bench with a back on it that I transfer onto from outside the shower stall. My husband would help me when he was home and preferred I didn't go in alone, since transferring was becoming an issue again. He helped me into the shower and went about his business, and I went about mine. I'm not sure how it happened, but the back of the chair snapped off and in the blink of an eye, I fell backwards.

I didn't actually "fall," but I hyperextended my entire body somehow. My butt was on the bench, my feet were on the floor in front of me, my head was on the floor behind me, and my belly was up in the air. I'm pretty sure that I blacked out, either from the trauma or possibly hitting my head on the shower wall. I also couldn't get myself back up. No matter how uncomfortable or painful it was, I was perfectly balanced. I was petrified—really afraid and started screaming.

My husband finally came in to check on me, even though he hadn't heard me yelling. I saw every ounce of color drain from his face and he froze. One look at me in that position through the glass door and he was sure I was dead. I started crying again and telling him to help me up, which he immediately did. He got me out of the shower, made sure I was okay, and instantly went into the garage, grabbed his screw gun, and put at least a dozen screws into the back of the chair in silence. I know now that that was his way of dealing with what he just saw.

He took me over to the doctor, and miraculously, I had managed to escape any injury, and so had the baby. It was a terrifying ordeal, and even though it really had nothing to do with me or anything I was doing, we made the decision that I shouldn't do too much transferring or moving around when I was home alone.

I hated having my independence taken away like that, but I was defeated. If it meant the safety of my child and of myself, I would do it. I was also still pretty freaked out by that one fall and was more willing than usual to accept some help.

CHAPTER 15

THE LAST COUPLE OF months of my pregnancy were pretty uneventful. I was scheduled for a C-section, and although I was worried about the actual birth and whatever consequences it could possibly bring, I was happy that we were much more prepared this time. My husband and I had also decided to have my tubes tied. After the three pregnancies and the physical toll they had taken on my body, we determined if we wanted another child in the future, we would be adopting.

The doctors prepped me for surgery and I was visibly shaking. Even though I thought I was prepared, it was still nerve-wracking. Being a paraplegic, I run the risk of something called "autonomic dysreflexia," and of course the doctors had to remind me of that right before the procedure. A basic explanation of autonomic dysreflexia is that parts of my body that I can't feel will be in extreme pain, but the message will not translate to my brain, leading to potentially life-threatening hypertension—not something I wanted to think about.

I was taken into the operating room with my husband by my side and awaited the birth of our new child. Our big fan club was again nervously waiting to hear what was happening, and I think even they were more anxious than expected. In a short time, the doctor had announced the birth of our baby boy! We were ecstatic and surprised, considering we really thought we were having a girl. He was healthy and beautiful and I had made it through once again unscathed and in much better shape than the first time around.

The doctor continued to work on me, performing the tubal, which took much longer than expected, so no one was able to go out and tell our families in the waiting room that we had a boy and everything was okay. They were very much relieved when my husband came out and first told our son he had a baby brother, and then made the announcement to everyone else.

After the surgery, I had to recover in the hospital for three to four days with my new baby. I was much more prepared this time and right away requested no medications other than over-the-counter painkillers, if needed. With my first son, I was put on morphine after his birth and was very out of it and oblivious to the fact that I was even medicated until a couple of days later.

It's not that I am immune to the pain, but I prefer to be cognizant. I also found it much easier to heal, knowing in advance what to expect and being able to move around. I was ready to leave after the second day, and on day three, I was sent home with my new baby.

It was a very stressful time for us—having a new business, a new baby, and a toddler to care for. Like any other parent with more than one child, I had to master tending to a newborn while considering the needs of an older child, who was not too thrilled about having a baby in the house to compete with. I had the advantage of already going through the learning process with my older son, but now I had to determine how to get around with both of them!

At that time, I drove a modified minivan, which had no middle row of seats and a ramp that would fold out of the passenger side door so I could maneuver in and out. I chose to switch to a van from my car when my first son was a baby because I just couldn't figure out how to get him in and out of the backseat. I had become somewhat of an expert of managing him when it came to the van. With all the extra space, I was able to move around and get him into his car seat. I also kept a large weight belt in the car to tie him to me when he was very little or when he was sleeping so I could easily use my hands to go up or down the ramp without having to balance him on my lap.

When my second came along, I encountered some new issues. He was an infant and needed to sit in a rear-facing car seat. I was completely unable to get him into the seat that way. He wasn't able yet to help me manipulate him to where he had to be and my balance wasn't good enough to hold him up and put him over and strap him in. I was in a bind, because I now had my older son who had places to go like school or activities and I was his transportation. My family offered to help—and they did for a while—but I had to come up with some way to do it myself.

Once again, my husband and I started brainstorming to come up with solutions. If my van had a middle row, I would be able to get in the right position to put the baby in the seat, but then I wouldn't be able to get into the van. It took a while, but we deduced that if we could have one single seat in the middle, even though it would be tight for me, I could do it.

Because of safety issues and regulations, it was near impossible to find anyone with the licensing and the know-how to design what we needed. Someone then referred me to a local team that built racecars. I brought in my van, showed him what we wanted done, and a few days later, they had constructed a safe and effective middle seat for me! I gave it a couple of tries strapping in my baby and off I went—free again.

It seemed there was very rarely an easy resolution for what I needed or wanted. Often I had to find a way on my own or with the help of those around me. But as they say, "where there's a will, there's a way." I didn't want to give up or accept that that something couldn't be done. There won't always be a solution to your problems, within yourself or outside in your surroundings, but that doesn't mean there is nothing that can be done. With the desire, determination, and the right resources, almost anything can be accomplished.

CHAPTER 16

AS MY YOUNGER SON approached his first month, I had to start thinking about getting back to work. As much as I hated the thought of leaving my babies, our business was getting busier and I was needed. I started back part-time before our son was a couple of months old. Things were a little hectic with working and taking care of children, but it had started to become our normal routine.

Just about the time my son was six months old, I got sick. I was pretty sure it was a urinary tract infection and saw the doctor, who gave me an antibiotic and I was on my way. Less than two weeks later, I was sick again. I had a very high fever, symptoms of a UTI, and an overall malaise. This time my doctor sent me to a urologist to be tested and see what was going on.

I went to my appointment, where they tested my urine and gave me an antibiotic. A few days later, I received a call from the doctor that the bacteria I had was resistant to the medication he gave me and I would need to take another. I felt better for a week or so, and then it started again. The doctor sent me for some further testing and found that I had kidney stones. I had developed some through my second pregnancy, but they were nothing to be concerned about at the time. They deduced that now these stones were harboring bacteria, and in order to permanently rid my body of this infection, I would have to have them removed.

The following week, I felt the onset of another fever and my doctor performed a surgery called lithotripsy. This procedure is done by pulverizing the kidney stones to allow them to break up and pass naturally through the urinary tract. I came home the night of the surgery with a very high fever, feeling worse than before, and I was advised to take more antibiotics.

A couple of days later I felt terrible. My symptoms seemed to be getting worse and my fever was getting higher. I decided to see my primary care doctor, since the urologist didn't seem very concerned. She sent me for a CAT scan, and before I even got home from the test, she called my cell phone and told me I needed to go to the hospital. She said I had a massive amount of bacteria built up in my kidneys and required treatment immediately.

I came home and told my husband and mother, packed a bag, and went to meet my doctor at the hospital to be admitted. When I got there, they also ran some additional tests and put me on intravenous antibiotics to rid my body of the infectious bacteria. I remained in the hospital hooked up to an IV for almost a week before they allowed me to go back home. Within a couple of weeks, the infection was back. My doctor put me on antibiotics again and advised me to see an infectious disease doctor.

So began the saga that I endured for almost two years. The infectious disease doctor found the same issue with the bacteria, and since I was sick again, admitted me back into the hospital for more intravenous antibiotics. I was miserable. I wanted to be home with my children and my husband. Once the medicine kicked in I felt fine, and it was emotionally draining to be sitting in a hospital bed when I just wanted to be home.

I continuously called the doctor's office to see what could be done. They agreed to put a port into my upper arm and send me home, where I would continue to have an antibiotic drip. I had to have a nurse come a few times and explain and show me how to do it, and then I was on my own.

I had no choice, since without the medicine I would be sick. I was happy to be out of the hospital, but it was agonizing sitting in front of my children, hooked up to an IV pole for over two hours each day. I did not want my boys seeing me like that. I also didn't like the state of mind it put me in where I was depressed and sad and just not myself. They deserved better than that, and so did I.

After about four more weeks of the in-home drip, the doctor finally removed the port and hoped everything would be okay. It wasn't long before it began again and I was frightened. I really didn't understand what was wrong anymore. I knew they thought it was caused by my kidneys, but nothing was helping me. No matter how much medication they pumped into my body, it kept coming back. I actually got to the point where I was afraid I was going to die. If the infectious disease doctor wasn't able to help me, who would be? Did they even know for sure what was going on? Was it ever going to stop?

I had a complete breakdown one night with my husband. I was hysterical to the point I could barely breathe. I didn't know how to help myself get better, and apparently, neither did the doctors. I couldn't take any more rounds of antibiotics, because once I was done with one, I would need a different one. It had become a never ending cycle for almost a year at that point, and I was honestly afraid I was going to die.

I called the infectious disease doctor the following day to let them know I was sick again. The doctor I spoke to told me to go to the hospital to be admitted and start another course of antibiotics—I refused. I tried to calmly explain that I didn't want to mask my symptoms anymore. Someone needed to figure out what the cause was, because obviously the antibiotics were not helping in the long run. He didn't like that answer and told me he couldn't help me if I didn't want to be helped. I had to go to the hospital or there was nothing he could do. I informed him that there was no way I was going back and if he wasn't willing to do something else, I guess our time together was coming to an end.

I contacted an old friend, who happened to be a urologist, for some advice. He listened to my frantic rant and advised me to see a urologist he worked with who was well-known in his field. He set me up with an appointment and we met shortly after.

I was thankful for the opportunity—finally, someone who wanted to get to the root of the problem. After speaking with me, looking into my records, and viewing my CAT scans and other diagnostics, he decided to try a new procedure. He was going to perform a surgery where he would go into my kidney with a scope and pull out the stones that he believed were harboring the bacteria causing the infections.

Within a couple of weeks, I was scheduled for surgery and admitted to the hospital for a round of pre-surgical antibiotics. We met the morning of the procedure and he was hopeful that this would work and told my mother, who was waiting for me, that it would be a fairly quick and non-invasive procedure.

After almost three hours he came out to the waiting room to let my mother know that he was sorry and had tried his hardest. She almost fainted because thought he meant I was dead. Luckily I made it through, but there was too much scar tissue and twisting of the tubes they needed to access the stones, and even though they gave it their best shot, there was nothing they could do.

He was pretty disappointed, although I don't think anywhere near as defeated as I felt. If he was the best in his field, where was I going to go from here? We spoke for a while and he recommended a combination of medicine and vitamin C, both of which would be meant to acidify my urine and create an environment unfavorable for bacteria to grow. He hoped this would help, but told me I may have to live with an infection because apparently, some people just do.

I spiraled right back into a depression. I didn't want to continue treating the problem—I wanted to get rid of it. I didn't want to be on medicine for an indefinite amount of time, either. I didn't really have any other options at the time, so I did what he said until I could come up with something better. It didn't help and my symptoms continued. Quite honestly, I could have lived with the pain or discomfort, but the fevers and fatigue from the infection were debilitating. I went back to see him six weeks later and was still in the same condition.

He advised me to continue with the medicine and vitamin C and didn't have any other suggestions for me. There was a highly-invasive procedure where they could go into my kidneys through my back and try to remove the stones, but it involved a long recovery and wasn't guaranteed to work because of the placement of the stones. I was back to square one.

I decided to try the holistic route and see if I could get any help or relief from that. I made an appointment with a prominent holistic doctor and was impressed with the information and advice he gave me. I tried the natural remedy he concocted for me, but that wasn't helping me, either. I went to see him a couple more times, but unfortunately didn't see any improvement.

At this point, I really didn't know where to turn. I had tried everyone and everything I could think of and hadn't shown any progress. I had done a ton of my own research and decided to take matters into my own hands. I had done a lot of reading about healing naturally through nutrition and cleansing and decided to give it a try—it sure couldn't hurt.

The last doctor had advised me to create an acidic environment in my body, but from everything I had read, the exact opposite was true. I needed to create an alkaline state in my body, because supposedly, bacteria and disease can't live like that. After more research, I came upon a nutritional program sold through multilevel marketing. I was pretty skeptical at first, but since one of the main agendas of their products is to make an alkaline environment in the body, I decided to give it a try.

I went through a couple of weeks of incorporating it into my diet and tried a cellular cleanse that they make, as well. After about two weeks, my body began to change. I didn't have a sallow look from being weak and medicated anymore, and I saw a significant change in my symptoms. I continued with the program and also began to change the foods I was eating. A little over a month later, I felt completely different. I seemed to have alleviated all of the symptoms and felt like my old self again. I had more energy than I'd had in the last couple of years, and even though when I was tested I was still holding onto the bacteria, I felt fine. I wasn't experiencing fevers anymore, I had no more chills and sweats, no more fatigue—nothing. Changing my diet had changed everything.

I don't claim to know more than the doctors I went to for treatment. I do not know for sure if what helped me would help others as well, but it worked. After two years of battling this illness and treating it repeatedly with medication, a change in my nutrition and diet made more improvement than I could have ever imagined. I was not cured, but I was well on my way.

Going through the experience I did forced me do a lot of research on self-healing, nutrition, and also to dig deeper into myself. I found that I had a real interest in what I was learning and enjoyed experimenting with different theories and different foods. The more I learned, the more I wanted to know.

I started sharing what I was learning with family and friends. After listening to me talk about it for so long, a few even started heeding my advice. I was having a great time passing on the knowledge I had gathered, and even more so when I realized I was able to help people. It was at that point it hit me—I finally knew what my calling in life was! I wanted to help people. I wanted to help others learn to be healthy and happy.

Soon after, I enrolled in an integrative nutrition program. I learned an enormous amount of information and became a much better coach to others. I received my certification and began my career as a health and life coach. Being able to help others achieve acceptance and balance in their lives has been extremely rewarding. I know that many people have seen me as an inspiration of sorts, which for so long made me feel uncomfortable. I was finally able to use that quality others saw in me to help them get their lives back.

It was a big turning point for me, as well. When I was taking classes, I was also applying what I was learning to myself. I had become a living example of how this actually works. I loved being able to use my background in food and my new education in nutrition to help myself and others grow and improve. I had unknowingly helped so many people during the course of my life, and now I was looking forward to doing it for a living.

CHAPTER 17

I HAVE SEEN AND heard many people speak about their rough road to recovery and how their determination and perseverance helped push them through. Sometimes I would wonder if I had tried harder, or did something different, or chose different beliefs, maybe I could have been that person. Then I dream about being that person who overcame, the one who against all odds made a recovery, but that's not me—at least, not yet.

Wondering about what would have been or what might happen isn't helping me accomplish anything. I would love to live my life like a "normal" person—walking around, not worrying about the size of the next door, running with my children, doing all of the things I just can't do. But if that meant changing what I have, giving up the amazing people around me, and forgetting the crazy adventures I have been on—I wouldn't change a thing.

Sometimes in life, no matter how bad you want something or how hard you try, there is nothing you can do to change your situation. Instead of working to try to change things, put your efforts into making the best of the life you have. It may take a little creativity or actively training yourself to think differently, but it is possible, and once you get there, it can be incredible.

For many years after my accident, my only focus was how to walk again. Of course, I was also having fun with my friends and working and raising a family, but my main goal was learning to walk. I spent most of my free time in physical therapy and trying new and alternative forms of medicine. I was living a happy life, but I felt that it would never be complete unless I was walking. I would always think, "If I accept the way I am, I won't be able to change."

But there did come a point where I started to back off a little, where I needed to spend more time and energy getting the rest of my life going. My college workload was getting bigger, and of course, I had a busy social calendar! Therapy started to take a back seat, and without consciously thinking about it, walking through life was no longer as necessary as just living. I continued with physical therapy a couple of days a week and exercised on my own, and started to focus on the more important things in my life at that time, like school, work, and boys!

Without thinking about it, my life continued on. I was having a great time doing the things we all do and even taking more risks than I normally would have. I did some traveling, drove across country, and even went skydiving! It wasn't until very recently that I realized walking wasn't as significant as I always thought it had been.

I was food shopping with my sons and a woman stopped me. She said her son recently had a spinal cord injury and was having a very hard time with it. He was seeing a physical therapist that I had seen for years, and she had heard about me from her. She told me that the therapist said that I "gave up" and wanted to know if it was true. I was so angry! I was fuming, not at this woman in the supermarket, or even that people were talking about me in general, but that they were saying I quit. I nicely told her that I would never quit and her son could contact me at any time if he ever wanted to talk.

Me? Quit? What? It was at this point, almost twenty years later, that I realized what had happened. I had stopped trying to change what had happened to me and accepted it. I accepted who I was now: the same beautiful person, just sitting down. I was still me, whether I was walking or rolling, and accepting that was not quitting—it was the beginning of my life.

I will never give up hope for my physical situation to change but even if it doesn't, so what? I have a great life and am thankful for every day I am given. I have done things that many able-bodied people have not. I found out how important it is to accept yourself for who you are, not who you want to be, in order to live a fulfilling life.

Sometimes we need to let go of the past in order to move ahead. Things won't always be how we want them to be, but they can still be amazing. We need to be excited about life, and in order to do that, we need acceptance. Acceptance of who we are, what we have, and the talents and exceptional traits we possess. We need to stop trying to change and recreate what we think should be and forge ahead regardless to create the life we want. It may not be life the way you once thought it would be, but it is your life, and you have the power to make it as fun and incredible as you desire.